Dreadful Droughts

Heinemann Library
Chicago, Illinois

Louise and Richard Spilsbury

Customer Service 888-454-2279
Visit our website at www.heinemannlibrary.com

Designed by David Poole and Paul Myerscough
Originated by Dot Gradations Limited
Printed in Hong Kong, China by Wing King Tong

07 06 05 04 03
10 9 8 7 6 5 4 3 2 1

Library of Congress Cataloging-in-Publication Data
Spilsbury, Louise.
  Dreadful droughts / Louise and Richard Spilsbury.
     v. cm. -- (Awesome forces of nature)
Includes bibliographical references and index.
Contents: What is a drought? -- What causes droughts? -- Where do droughts happen? -- What happens in a drought? -- Case study: Eastern Australia, 1994 -- Who helps when droughts happen? -- Case study: United States, 2002 -- Can droughts be predicted? -- Can people prepare for droughts? -- Case study: Ethiopia, 1997 to 2002 -- Can droughts be prevented? -- Severe droughts of the twentieth century.
  ISBN 1-4034-3723-8 (lib. bdg.) -- ISBN 1-4034-4231-2 (pbk.)
  1. Droughts--Juvenile literature. 2. Droughts--Environmental aspects--Juvenile literature. [1. Droughts.] I. Spilsbury, Richard, 1963- II. Title.
  QC929.25.S65 2003
  363.34'929--dc21
                                         2003001108

Acknowledgments
The author and publisher are grateful to the following for permission to reproduce copyright material:
Cover photograph by Corbis.
p. 4 B. Gibbs/Trip; pp. 5, 11, 17, 19 SIPA Press/Rex Features; p. 6 Galen Rowell/ Corbis; p. 8 Dinodia/Trip, pp. 10, 28 Associated Press; pp. 12, 13, 22 Das Fotoarchive; p. 15 Paul A. Souders/ Corbis; p. 16 Still Pictures; p. 18 Clive Shirley/Panos Pictures; p. 21 Getty News and Sport; p. 23 Science Photo Library; p. 25 Eric Smith/Trip; p. 27 C. Steele Perkins/ Magnum.

Some words are shown in bold, **like this.** You can find out what they mean by looking in the glossary.

Contents

What Is a Drought?

A drought happens when little or no rain falls for a long time in an area that usually gets rain. It badly affects the lives and health of the plants, people, and other animals living there. All living things depend on water in some way. Our bodies are mostly made up of water, and we cannot live without water for longer than a few days.

Plants need water to grow properly and animals need water to drink. We use water to cook our food, to keep clean, and to carry away our waste. Water is used to make electricity for homes, factories, and power plants. Factories also use water to cool and clean machinery. When there is a shortage of water, all of these things are affected.

Not all droughts are deadly. A minor drought during the summer may simply mean that people have to water their lawns and **crops.** *They can use stored or tap water while they wait for rain to come.*

Devastating droughts

A major drought is one that affects a large area and a great many living things for a very long time. Droughts in parts of Africa can last for years. Without enough water, farmers may not be able to grow crops for several years in a row. People and their **livestock** have so little food to eat that they become sick and may die.

Drought is serious in poorer countries, such as Somalia in Africa. Poor people do not have enough money to buy food and water, and their government may not be able to help them.

What Causes Droughts?

Droughts happen when not enough rain falls on an area of land. It may still rain once in a while. However, the rain that falls dries up quickly afterwards and does not really help.

What causes rain?

When water on the surface of the world's oceans and rivers warms up, it evaporates. This means that warm air turns it from liquid water into a gas in the air that we cannot see, called water **vapor.** When a patch of air gets pushed high into the air the water vapor in it cools down again. The water vapor turns back into droplets of water. They are so small and light that they float in the air and cling to tiny bits of dust in the air. Clumps of these droplets gather together to form clouds that we can see. Eventually the water droplets become so large and heavy that they fall from the clouds as rain.

A cloud is a large mass of very tiny droplets of water.

Why does it stop raining?

Water vapor only turns back into droplets of water if the air it is in rises into the colder parts of the sky. If the air does not rise, then no clouds form. Without clouds, there is no rain.

Air rises and falls depending on **air pressure.** Most people have heard weather **forecasters** talk about high- and low-**pressure systems.** It is a difficult subject, but basically when there is high air pressure, air does not rise. Air only rises when there is low air pressure.

What is air pressure?

Sometimes the air above Earth is pushed together. Scientists call this a high-pressure system. It brings clear, dry weather. Other times the air is not quite so pushed together. This is a low-pressure system. It brings cloudy, rainy weather.

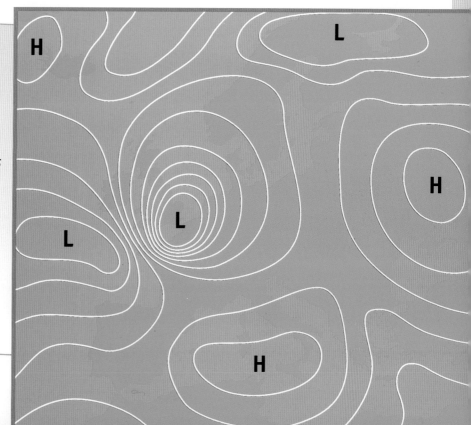

The lines on this weather map show pressure systems over Europe. High-pressure systems are marked "H" and low-pressure systems are marked "L." These systems are constantly moving and changing. Weather is usually wet in low-pressure areas, and dry in high-pressure areas.

Pressure systems

High-**pressure systems** and low-pressure systems usually move around. Therefore, most countries get some rainy days and some dry days. Sometimes high-pressure systems stay over the same place for a long time. They may be held in place by wide, fast-moving air **currents** high in the sky.

Sometimes, cold or warm water currents in the oceans can change the way the wind moves. These water currents can also stop pressure systems from moving on. For example, a giant warm current called **El Niño** can keep high-pressure systems over countries in Asia, such as India. When a high-pressure system stays too long, it can cause drought.

In parts of Asia, summer winds usually blow rain clouds like these north from the Indian Ocean. As the clouds pass over land they bring the monsoon season—when it rains almost every day for many weeks. If the rain clouds do not come, there is drought.

Where Do Droughts Happen?

Droughts can happen in nearly any area of land in the world. They happen most often in places with hot and dry **climates,** such as parts of Africa, the United States, Australia, and India. Droughts happen less often in places with wetter climates, like Scandinavia and the North and South **Poles.**

Droughts cause the most problems in places where people need lots of water for their **crops** to grow or for their **livestock** to drink. In some of these places, such as southern parts of the U.S., droughts ruin huge areas of crops. Droughts are bad for farmers because it means they make less money than usual. In other places, such as Somalia in Africa, droughts can result in people starving. When their food plants and animals die, poor people have nothing to eat. They may die unless they are given help.

The red patches on this map show the areas on Earth which receive the least rain. When droughts happen, they affect dry areas worse than wet areas.

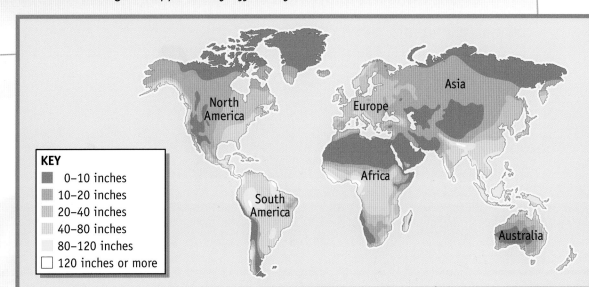

KEY
- 0–10 inches
- 10–20 inches
- 20–40 inches
- 40–80 inches
- 80–120 inches
- 120 inches or more

What Happens in a Drought?

The first signs of drought are when grass turns brown and other plants **wilt.** As **groundwater** dries up, cracks appear across the land.

After a few weeks, plants start to die. When plant roots shrivel, they no longer hold the soil together. The soil is then **eroded** by wind. Sometimes enough dust gets blown into the air to form giant dust storms. Bare patches of soil get hotter than those covered in plants. In some places, **wildfires** may start. These fires will spread quickly through any remaining dry plants.

Affecting future crops

Topsoil is the top layer of soil on the ground. It is more fertile (good for growing **crops**) than the soil below. If wind and rain erode topsoil, the soil that is left is less fertile. This means that future crops cannot grow so well.

Droughts can last for more than five or even ten years.

Animals in a drought

During a drought, animals cannot find enough to drink or to eat. They may also suffer from heat stroke—a sickness caused by getting too hot. As plants die, plant-eating animals, such as wildebeest or sheep, have to travel farther to find food. As they move, they erode the dry soil with their hooves. Many of these animals die of hunger and **dehydration.** Then carnivores— animals that eat other animals, such as lions—cannot catch enough prey and they begin to starve.

Some animals benefit from the death of other animals. **Scavengers,** such as hyenas and vultures, eat dead animals. However, the bodies of dead animals are also places where **bacteria** grow. When flies feed on the bodies, they pick up bacteria and spread diseases to other animals.

In times of drought, all animals are at risk of dying of dehydration—when they do not have enough water for their bodies to work properly.

Lakes, reservoirs, and rivers

During a drought, the water levels in lakes, **reservoirs,** and rivers are low. Animals that live there have fewer places to breed (have babies) or take shelter. When rivers or streams stop flowing into lakes and reservoirs, the water becomes **stagnant.** Fish and other animals that breathe oxygen in water then suffocate (die from lack of oxygen).

Using less water

People in villages, towns, and cities have to use less water in a drought. They must have enough water to drink. So, they have to reduce how much water they use for cooking and how often they wash themselves or flush their toilets. Factories and **power plants** also have to limit the amount of water they use.

Some plants, called algae, thrive in stagnant water. They can take over lakes and reservoirs. They may also produce poisons that kill animals and other plants that share the water.

Famine

A **famine** is when a large number of people do not have enough to eat. Famine is often the result of a serious drought. When drought kills crops and plants that **livestock** usually eat, many poor people go hungry. If people do not have enough food they become weak and may die from **malnutrition.** If there is not enough clean water, they may have to drink any dirty water they can find. This means they may catch diseases that cause **diarrhea** and dehydration.

If their livestock dies, people affected by drought may have nothing to sell in order to buy food.

Eastern Australia, 1994

Australia is one of the driest continents on Earth. Because of this dryness, drought is a part of Australia's **climate** and the government does not usually consider it to be a natural disaster, except in extraordinary circumstances such as those in 1994. That year, conditions in eastern Australia were among the driest since people began keeping records. A large part of the country officially had its worst drought of the twentieth century.

The cause of the drought was warm **El Niño** sea **currents** off South America that changed the movement of winds across a large area. This change meant rain clouds were not blown over eastern Australia from the Pacific Ocean. Some rain did fall, but not nearly as much as usual. **Reservoirs** and rivers dried up, and water had to be delivered to many towns in the countryside for up to a year.

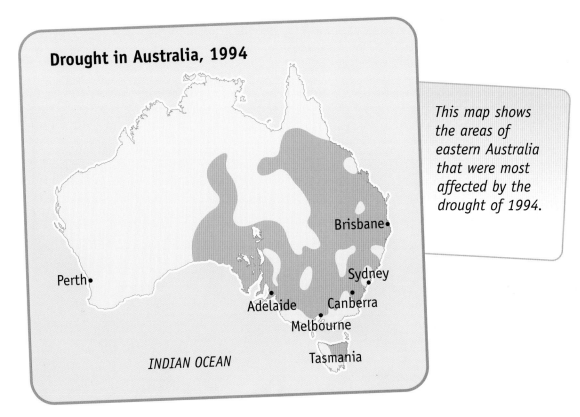

Drought in Australia, 1994

This map shows the areas of eastern Australia that were most affected by the drought of 1994.

Drought damages

The drought damaged many wild plants and killed large areas of **crops** and **pasture.** Then, the price of animal foods, such as grain, went up. So, farmers could not afford to keep much **livestock.** Life for farmers became impossible. They had fewer cattle and sheep to sell and had more food to buy for those animals. Many farmers were forced to give up. They went to live and work in big towns.

> "The worst thing is we have lost neighbors on both sides. They were not only neighbors but were our friends." A Queensland farmer

Moving wildlife

When there are fewer plants to eat, wild animals come into towns looking for food. Thousands of wild mice ruined large areas of crops worth millions of dollars as they traveled across farmland.

At one point, 30 families a week were leaving their farms forever because they could not afford to live on them any longer.

Who Helps when Droughts Happen?

A drought is a natural event like an **earthquake.** The difference between a drought and most other natural events is that a drought builds up very slowly. People need more help as the drought continues.

Rich and poor

Droughts affect wealthy countries less than poor countries because

- they can afford to store larger amounts of food and water;
- they have more pipes and canals, and more vehicles to transport water when it runs out;
- they can buy food if their supplies run out or if **crops** fail;
- people have more radios and TVs to receive drought warnings;
- they can afford larger **emergency services** and armed forces with better equipment to help when a drought hits;
- richer governments can afford to help farmers affected by drought.

Poor people may rely on wells for their water and have few other places to get clean water.

Rationing

When water and food are in short supply, people must be careful that it does not run out. Government workers do this by rationing, or controlling the amount that each person can use. At first, rations are generous. If a drought goes on for a long time, they become smaller. For example, rationing at the beginning of a drought may mean people can use water normally except that they cannot water their lawns. Later on, rations may only be enough for essential uses—drinking, cooking, and some washing. When stored water runs out, it has to be brought in from elsewhere.

Extreme rationing

In some countries, police fine or even imprison people who use more than their share of water. In severe droughts, the army or police sometimes guard water wells and food supplies.

In the 1989 drought in England, some people had to get their water from tanks in the street.

On the move

Poor people often have to move away from places that are badly affected by drought. They travel to areas where they can find food and water. These people are known as **refugees.** When many refugees gather in one place, they use up the stored food and water there. Often, refugees are too weak to travel any further.

Local emergency services and **volunteers** give out rations of food and water. They may also provide some medical care and shelter for the refugees. Usually they also need help from other countries.

Emergencies

The police, fire department, ambulance services, and army have to help when drought causes other problems. For example, **firefighters** have to put out forest fires that burn dry trees. Medical workers treat people for the effects of smoke and heat from the fires.

Refugees usually take as many of their possessions as they can with them when they move to escape a threat such as drought.

Types of aid

The help that people give to those in need is called **aid.** Money, food, medicines, blankets, and clothes are all types of aid. Governments and large organizations in other countries often send aid to countries in need. People like you also give aid by sending donations (gifts of money) to local, national, or international **charities.** After a big drought, charities such as the Red Cross or Oxfam make special requests, asking for donations so they can help people in need quickly.

There are different kinds of aid. For example, charities may provide new trucks to bring water or food to people who need it. Or, they may send tools and materials so people can dig better wells for themselves. They may also send equipment to build larger **reservoirs** to store more water for future droughts.

*In times of drought, trained medical workers can help to treat **malnutrition** or **dehydration.***

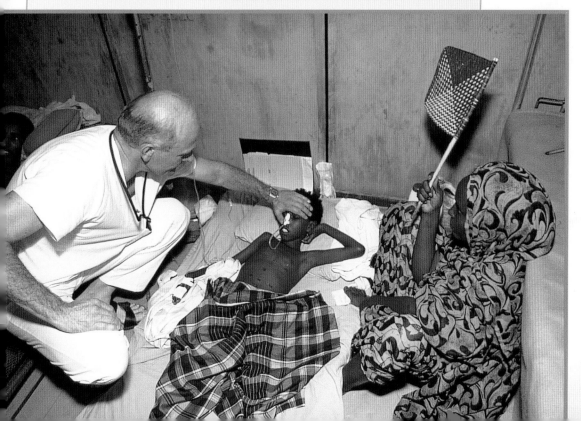

United States, 1998 to 2002

From 1998 to 2002, far less rain and snow than usual fell over large areas of the United States. In some parts, a whole year's worth of rain did not arrive, so rivers, lakes, and **reservoirs** dried up. By summer 2002, about one-third of the United States was experiencing a severe drought.

Plants were extremely dry, winds were strong, and temperatures were high. These were ideal conditions for **wildfires.** There were at least twice as many wildfires as usual. Several states coped with the fires by hiring extra **firefighters** and buying extra fire-fighting equipment such as airplanes that drop water.

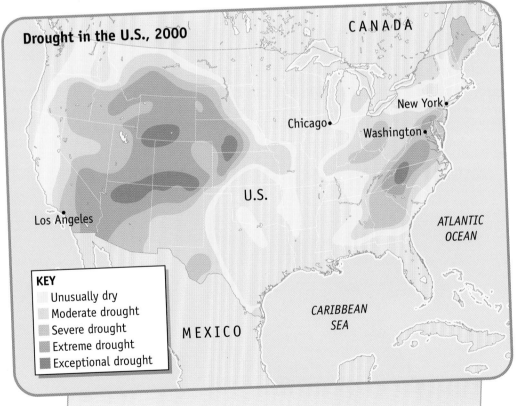

Drought in the U.S., 2000

CANADA

New York

Chicago

Washington

U.S.

Los Angeles

ATLANTIC OCEAN

KEY
Unusually dry
Moderate drought
Severe drought
Extreme drought
Exceptional drought

MEXICO

CARIBBEAN SEA

In summer 2000, many parts of the United States suffered extreme drought conditions. The worst affected areas are shown in red. The drought lasted until 2002.

Saving water

In Maine, half of the people in the countryside get their water from shallow wells. Many of these wells dried up during the drought. Most people could not afford to dig deeper wells to reach deeper **groundwater.** Many had to drive trucks into towns to fill containers with water. They had to conserve (save) water in any way they could.

> "We started using paper plates to eat off and using our pasta water to flush the toilet. I even rinsed my hair in the dog's drinking bucket."
> Cynthia Novacek, Maine

Saving water in towns and cities was just as important. New York usually uses one billion gallons of water a year. In the drought, businesses were supplied with less water. People were ordered not to use water to wash pavements or cars or to water lawns, especially during the hotter parts of the day.

During the drought, New York public fountains like this one were shut down to remind people about the need to conserve water.

Can Droughts Be Predicted?

The cost of dealing with the effects of drought can be great. Therefore, many people try to predict when they may strike, so that preparations can be made in advance. People make predictions by studying **climate** and weather patterns.

Past climate

Have you ever seen the growth rings on cut-down trees or logs? Similar rings can be seen in **coral.** One of the ways scientists know about climate in the past is by looking at these rings. Both trees and coral grow more in wet years, producing wider rings. They grow less in dry years, which means the rings are narrower.

Growth rings suggest that droughts happen in cycles (repeated patterns). In Australia, they happen on average every eighteen years. If people know how long the drought cycle in a country is, they can predict when a drought is likely to happen next.

By looking at the pattern of growth rings in trees, scientists can figure out when there were extremely dry years in the past.

Weather

Scientists predict droughts by figuring out how the weather will affect the land. They measure and record how hot it is and how much rain or snow falls. They also measure how high the water is in rivers and **reservoirs** and how dry the soil is. They use **satellites** in space and aircraft to take photos of rain clouds all over the Earth. By measuring the speed and direction of the wind and the **air pressure,** they can figure out how fast and where **pressure systems** are moving.

Using all of this information, they can **forecast** the weather up to a month in advance. They predict drought by working out how climate patterns and weather will affect the amounts of water in rivers, reservoirs, **groundwater,** and soil.

*Weather in one place can affect weather thousands of miles away. For example, warm **El Niño currents** (the red areas in the middle of the Pacific Ocean in the picture) make some places dry and other places wet.*

Can People Prepare for Droughts?

Some countries try to plan for the next drought before it happens. They do not want to wait and try to deal with it afterward. Their governments make plans by knowing about the water they have—how much is used and how much is stored. Governments study what effects a drought would have in different areas.

Planning for the future

In some places, drought would mean **famine** for the people who live there. In these places, planning might mean storing more food. In other areas, dried-up rivers might mean that fewer tourists would visit and spend money in shops and hotels. Part of a drought plan might be encouraging new businesses to start up so local people do not rely too heavily on money from tourism.

*In Australia, rainfall maps like this are posted on the Internet. These maps help farmers plan what **crops** to plant or how many **livestock** to raise at particular times of year.*

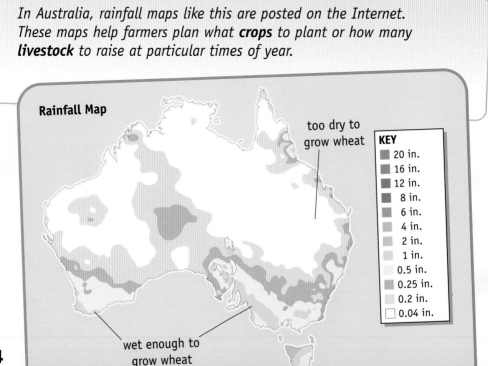

Rainfall Map

too dry to grow wheat

KEY
- 20 in.
- 16 in.
- 12 in.
- 8 in.
- 6 in.
- 4 in.
- 2 in.
- 1 in.
- 0.5 in.
- 0.25 in.
- 0.2 in.
- 0.04 in.

wet enough to grow wheat

Planning for less water

The best way to plan for drought is to use less water now. Using less water means rivers and **reservoirs** will be fuller. In our homes, we can do this in many ways. We can turn off the tap when we brush our teeth or buy a dishwasher that uses less water. City planners can plant smaller lawns that need less watering and encourage people to collect and store rainwater.

Farmers can plan for drought by growing **drought-tolerant** crops. These are crops that can survive a drought, either because they need less water or have long roots that can reach underground water. They can also raise livestock that are able to thrive with less water. Some farmers can build better **irrigation** canals so crops can be watered more easily.

*In Queensland, Australia, some farmers plant salt bush plants. Salt bush can grow when it is too dry for **pasture**, and it provides useful **protein** for their sheep.*

Ethiopia, 1997 to 2002

Ethiopia is a poor country where people have suffered badly from many droughts. Recently, they have had droughts for eight years in a row.

Now, Ethiopian people—with **aid** from other countries, organizations, and **charities**—are working to be better prepared when the next drought strikes. For example, they are gathering bigger supplies of food and water. They are working on better drought prediction. They are also creating new health clinics so that young and elderly people will be stronger and better able to survive hard times.

DROUGHT FACTS

! Drought and **famine** have affected African countries, such as Ethiopia, more seriously than anywhere else on Earth.

! From the 1960s to 1970s, millions of people suffered and about 30 million **livestock** died.

! Many African countries were also affected by a massive drought in the 1980s to 1990s.

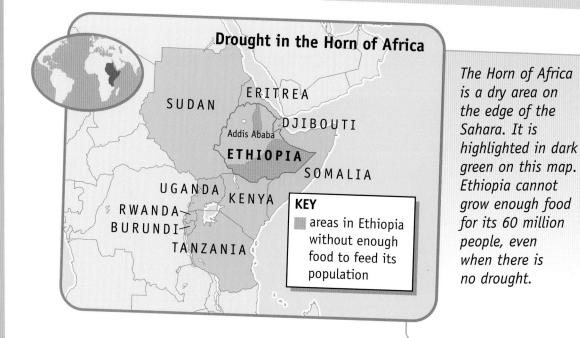

Drought in the Horn of Africa

SUDAN

ERITREA

DJIBOUTI

Addis Ababa

ETHIOPIA

SOMALIA

UGANDA KENYA

RWANDA

BURUNDI

TANZANIA

KEY

■ areas in Ethiopia without enough food to feed its population

The Horn of Africa is a dry area on the edge of the Sahara. It is highlighted in dark green on this map. Ethiopia cannot grow enough food for its 60 million people, even when there is no drought.

Changing traditions

Traditionally, many people in the Horn of Africa were nomads. Nomads are people who move around with their animals to places with **pasture** and water. They also look for places with trees and bushes so they can use the wood for cooking.

In droughts, there are only a few areas with healthy plants. Many nomads move their cattle and goats to these areas. With so much use, the plants in these places die and the soil **erodes.**

The Ethiopian government and aid workers are working to encourage nomads to take care of the land—for example, by teaching them to control where their animals graze. The government helps by planting **drought-tolerant crops.** It also provides the nomads with stoves that use less wood for cooking and heating than normal ones.

In 2002 in Ethiopia, drought planning, such as storing food aid like this, meant fewer people were affected by drought than in the past. Even so, millions of people suffered from **malnutrition.**

Can Droughts Be Prevented?

Droughts are awesome forces of nature that we cannot prevent. But we can help prevent the suffering that droughts bring to people's lives by predicting droughts earlier. We can also be better prepared for the problems caused by droughts.

Taking care

We also need to be careful not to make things worse. Many people believe that temperatures around the world are gradually increasing. Higher temperatures make dry places even drier and more likely to have droughts. They say the change is caused by the greenhouse effect. When we burn fuels such as oil we release gases into the air. These gases form a layer in the air that traps heat from the sun, just as a greenhouse does. Many scientists believe that we should use fuel more carefully, to slow the warming of the Earth. Otherwise future droughts could be even worse than they are now.

We should all treat water as a precious resource and not as something we can waste.

Severe Droughts of the Past 100 Years

1907 and 1936, China
The worst drought in history happened in the Yangtze river valley in 1907. Drought and **famine** killed an estimated 24 million people. Another five million died from drought and famine in 1936.

1921–1922, Soviet Union
Drought in the Volga river region caused famine from 1921 to 1922. Tens of millions of people starved and as many as five million died.

1930–1939, United States
During the 1930s, fifteen states had their lowest rainfall and highest temperatures in decades. **Crops** failed and **topsoil eroded,** causing massive dust storms that blew across the land, choking people and animals. Hundreds of thousands left their farms as **refugees**.

1965–1973, Horn of Africa
For these eight years, no rain fell and 200,000 people died in northeastern Africa. Further droughts in the 1980s and 1990s, combined with the effects of war, created millions of refugees and killed hundreds of thousands.

1965–1967 and 1987–1988, India
In 1965–1967 drought caused crop failure, and famine killed around 1.5 million people. In 1987–1988 drought affected larger areas but killed far fewer people because India was better prepared.

2000–2002, United States
Large areas in the Rocky Mountain and southeastern regions of the United States had drought in 2000. The droughts caused great difficulties for farmers and increased the number of **wildfires.** These conditions continued until 2002.

Glossary

aid help that is given, such as money, medicine, food, or other necessary items

air pressure measurement of how strongly different bits of air push against each other

bacteria tiny living things that can cause diseases

charity group that gives out aid to the poor and suffering

climate weather patterns that happen over several years

coral hard substance formed by the skeletons of tiny sea creatures over many years

crop plant grown by people for food or other uses

current movement of water or air in particular directions

dehydration when a creature's body does not have enough water

diarrhea sickness that causes watery bowel movements and leads to dehydration

drought-tolerant able to grow in drought conditions

earthquake shaking of the ground caused by large movements inside the Earth

El Niño warm water current in the Pacific Ocean that affects climate elsewhere

emergency service government-run service such as the police, fire department, or ambulance services

eroded worn away by wind, water, or rubbing

famine when large numbers of people do not have enough food

firefighter man or woman who works for the fire department, fighting fires

forecast predict. A weather forecaster is someone who predicts the weather.

groundwater water found in soil or in cracks in rocks

irrigation building canals and channels to give water to plants

livestock animals kept by people to eat or to sell

malnutrition sickness caused by not eating enough of the right foods

pasture grass for livestock to eat

pole North Pole or South Pole—the most northerly or southerly place on Earth. They poles are covered in thick ice.

power plant factory that makes electricity

pressure system area with high or low pressure that affects the weather. In a low-pressure system air rises, creating clouds and rain; in a high-pressure system air falls, so no clouds form and the land below gets dry weather.

protein type of chemical that people and animals need to eat in order to survive. Meat and beans are two types of food containing protein.

refugee person who moves to escape danger such as drought or war

reservoir large, natural or man-made lake used to store water

satellite machine put into space by people to do jobs such as sending out TV signals or taking photographs

scavenger animal that eats dead animals
stagnant stale water that does not move, running out of oxygen
topsoil upper layer of soil that soaks up groundwater and is ideal for growing crops
vapor gas such as steam that turns to liquid once it cools
volunteer person who offers help without being paid
wildfire natural fire affecting dry plants
wilt go limp because of dryness

More Books to Read

Bundey, Nikki. *Drought and People*. Minneapolis: Lerner Publishing, 2001.

Jennings, Terry. *Droughts*. North Mankato, Minn.: Thameside Press, 1999.

Stein, Paul. *Droughts of the Future*. New York: Rosen Publishing Group, 2001.

Ylvuaker, Anne. *Droughts*. Mankato, Minn.: Capstone Press, 2003.

Index